Cheerful Inspirations

Uplifting Words
to Color and Display

ZENDOODLE COLORSCAPES: CHEERFUL INSPIRATIONS.
Copyright © 2019 by St. Martin's Press. All rights reserved.
Printed in Canada. For information, address
St. Martin's Press, 175 Fifth Avenue, New York, N.Y. 10010.

www.stmartins.com
www.castlepointbooks.com

The Castle Point Books trademark is owned by Castle Point Publishing, LLC.
Castle Point books are published and distributed by St. Martin's Press.

ISBN 978-1-250-23039-3 (trade paperback)

Our books may be purchased in bulk for promotional, educational, or business use.
Please contact your local bookseller or the Macmillan Corporate and Premium
Sales Department at 1-800-221-7945, extension 5442, or by email
at MacmillanSpecialMarkets@macmillan.com.

First Edition: June 2019

10 9 8 7 6 5 4 3 2 1

zendoodle colorscapes

Cheerful Inspirations

Uplifting Words to Color and Display

CASTLE POINT BOOKS

NEW YORK

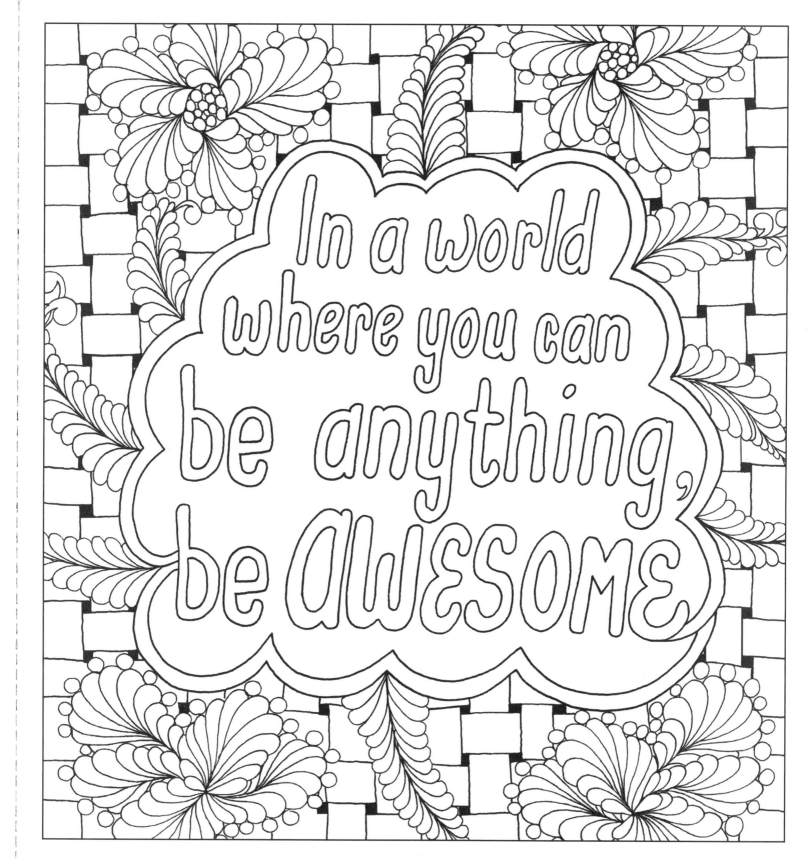